THE *Archive Photographs* SERIES

NORTH NORFOLK

The old three-funnel *HMS Norfolk*, when she visited the resorts of Cromer and Great Yarmouth about sixty years ago. *HMS Norfolk* was adopted by Norwich during the Second World War. Her flags and ensign, which she flew when she fired the first shot marking the end of the Scharnhorst, were presented to Norwich and now hang in Blackfriars Hall.

THE
Archive Photographs
SERIES

NORTH NORFOLK

Compiled by
Cliff Richard Temple

First published 1995

The Chalford Publishing Company
St Mary's Mill, Chalford,
Stroud, Gloucestershire, GL6 8NX

ISBN 0 7524 0149 1

Typesetting and origination by
The Chalford Publishing Company
Printed in Great Britain by
Redwood Books, Trowbridge

The Victorian method of baby transportation.

Contents

Introduction

North Norfolk has a charm of its own, surprising many people in its versatility, ranging from quaint narrow streets (so pleasing to the eye), to magnificent ruins dating from Roman times – fortresses, priories, encampments, and Norman castles.

Round-tower Saxon churches greet one, so do picturesque thatched churches. As a complete contrast are the various bird sanctuaries, Norfolk being the first county in England to establish its own nature reserve. For many years now, the towns of Cromer and Sheringham have been popular as holiday resorts, catering for a clientele who do not relish the razzmatazz of Blackpool. Eighteenth-century Cromer acquired a reputation as a health resort, Clement Scott helping to bring in the gentry through writing a poem, *The Gardens of Sleep*, from the mass of poppies growing on the cliff tops. Cromer is also known for its mouth-watering crabs (caught by the catcher!) and not least for the courage and wonderful seamanship of its lifeboat coxswain, Cox Henry Blogg, who rescued unfortunate mariners from mines, torpedoes and rough weather shipwrecks (1876–1954) gaining more awards than any other lifeboatman: Lifeboat V.C. – Gold Medal – three times; silver, four times; the George Cross and British Empire medal! Truly a wonderful man. Cromer has a terrace of tall Regency houses with a mid-Victorian hotel, the Hotel-de-Paris, with its brick turrets and copper domes.

Some six hundred years ago, Cromer was part of Shipden, but erosion swept the latter away. It is now under the sea, leaving Cromer secure with a huge sea wall. Many people raise their eyebrows when told that a passenger steam boat got wrecked on a church steeple, but such was the case, for on 9 August 1888 the steamer tug *Victoria* left Yarmouth with about one hundred passengers on board, for a day trip to Cromer. Having no pier, passengers were landed by means of the *Victoria*'s small boat. After a pleasant stay and look around Cromer, they returned to the vessel for the trip home. The engines were started, and the vessel moved forward, and then a ker-unch! was heard and felt! She had struck a rock, and was rapidly taking in water. Once more the passengers took to the small boat, aided by local fishermen in their boats, who had seen the mishap, and they were taken back to Yarmouth by train. For just a day or two, at low water, the locals did a good trade taking holidaymakers out to view the wreck. After many attempts at salvage the remaining debris was thought to be a danger, so an explosive was used to blow it up. With the ship went part of the rock, which was said to be the tower of the Shipden Church which had been covered by the sea for centuries. Thus a ship was wrecked on a church steeple!

For the greater part of the nineteenth century, lower Sheringham remained a fishing village and two lifeboats were established, and the fishermen who manned them saved many lives. Then towards the end of the century it was realised it had many advantages as a seaside resort, and new houses and streets sprang up in all directions. Thus Sheringham constituted two distinct parts – Lower and Marine Sheringham, the latter living on the harvest of the sea.

Sheringham was first mentioned in *Domesday Book*, but it was called Silingeham. It was given by William the Conqueror to William de Sconies as a reward for services rendered at the Battle of Hastings. It eventually passed into the possession of the Crown for fishing for cod, flats, crabs, and whelks. Visitors like it today because it is something different to so many summer resorts. Of special interest is the old pulling lifeboat, the *Henry Ramey Upcher*, now preserved for all time.

Within a mile or so is Pretty Corner, a wood containing evidence that it was once inhabited by Ancient Britons – the ancient pits that abound there are said to be the dwelling places of the Iceni. A near neighbour is Beeston Regis, which has quite a history of its own, being centred on the priory, which was founded during the reign of King John.

So many interesting places, historical and otherwise, are within a few miles of each other. One of them is Felbrigg Hall, which was presented to the nation by R.W. Ketton-Cremer, the famous biographer of Horace Walpole. Felbrigg's most distinguished occupant was William Wyndham, who was Pitt's Secretary of War during the Napoleonic Wars. Then there is the great priory of Binham, whose Norman nave is still used as the Parish Church.

Mundesley is a must for holidaymakers, having a wonderful stretch of sand and marram grass. Its name is probably Anglo-Saxon or Norse, and it is mentioned in *Domesday Book* as Muleslai. It was frequently visited by Nelson as a boy, who attended the nearby Paston Grammar School. Many ships have ended their lives on its shore line – mountainous seas crushing their very existence. Within walking distance is Paston windmill, which was once the summer residence of Mr McDougal, the flour and cake magnate, and certainly a 'beautifier of the landscape'.

Wells is another popular seaside spot for a day out, once having a wonderful picnic area under hundreds of pine trees, with a fine kiddies' boating lake called Abrahams Bosom, but alas the inrush of salt water from the 1953 sea surge killed off all the trees, so only a 'desert' remains today. Having a harbour, ships are often seen unloading goods for the adjacent warehouses. An unusual long walk and embankment takes one from the quay to the sea, where a fine building houses the new lifeboat, recently named by the Duchess of Kent. At the beginning of the 'long walk' is a memorial, showing a mast, anchor and lifebuoy, dedicated to eleven of the crew of a former lifeboat, which capsized in a gale after saving the crew of one ship and going to the rescue of another.

What must be one of the finest examples of antiquity and beauty is the massive ruin of Castle Acre, built by William de Warenne, who married William the Conqueror's daughter. At the time it must have been one of the biggest East Anglian fortresses. With the combination of a Norman castle, medieval church, a priory and a Saxon cemetery making it a worthwhile visit, the Priory is now a national monument and cared for by the Office of Works. With its refectory, cloisters, and church, it needs little imagination to visualise the monks of old, treading its many paths. Castle Rising was once an important port, and it remains one of Norfolk's prettiest villages. It is now a couple of miles from the sea, which deserted it many years ago. An impressive sight is the four square castle, standing within mighty earthworks rising to 112 feet. Part of the keep remains, the best stronghold of its kind in the country. A tourist attraction is the Bede House which Henry Howard, earl of Northampton, gave the town in the reign of James I. In this retreat live eleven old ladies and their governess, each having her own carved chair and bedspread. A sight, not to be forgotten, is to see a procession these old ladies going to church on a Sunday, wearing red cloaks, with the Howard badge and the 'steeple' (similar to Wales) hats of their founder's day. Bacton (now the 'King Pin' workshop of the North Sea Oil and Gas Industry), has the remains of a Priory, which in the Middle Ages was a priory of widespread fame: pilgrims came along to gaze on what was reputed to be a fragment of the Cross. King Henry III came to it as a pilgrim when it was new; the church in which he knelt was a noble shrine 200 feet long. Two centuries later, John Paston was buried here and the crowd, it is said, was so great that 'the reke of the torches of the dirge was so overpowering, that the Priory glazier had to remove panes of glass so that the mourners should not be suffocated'.

Stiffkey. Whenever this word is mentioned, two words come quickly to mind, 'Stewkey Blues' and Harold Davidson! The first is the name given to that succulent creature, the cockle, which it is said was far better than any other gathered in the nearby villages. Huge loads were brought ashore from the muddy flats, and dispatched for miles around to buyers, eagerly seeking the 'best cockles in the country'. The second name of course relates to the scandalous and amazing story of the downfall of a North Norfolk clergyman, who became world news. In 1906 he came to this small village, and at first was thought to be a saint, striving to save young girls from prostitution and degradation, doing much good on London's Dockland settlement. Returning home from service in the Great War 1914–18 he found his wife expecting a baby, of which he was not the father. Thus the marriage was at an end, and he threw himself more into his work in Soho. But complaints against him began to be heard in relation to some of his young ladies and his slackness in parish matters, Fleet Street editors began to get hold of various stories against him and a trial opened on 29 March 1932 where accusations against Davidson steadily increased, affairs becoming more sordid as the trial proceeded. When on July 8 the trial finally ended, he was declared guilty of 'systematically misbehaving himself with young women' and ordered to pay the costs. On October 21 a ceremony was held at the Norwich Cathedral, during which the Reverend Harold Davidson was 'removed, deposed and degraded'. He then 'took to the stage' as a variety act, and then became a fairground exhibit, sitting in a barrel on the Promenade at Blackpool, proclaiming his innocence to the many holidaymakers who paid tuppence a time to look at him. From there he went to Skegness, where he took the part of Daniel in the lion's den, when on a fateful day, 28 July, he was mauled by one of the lions, dying two days later from injuries received.

Palling is a fishing village on a very perilous shore, having at one time two lifeboats installed. It has evidence of a history of over a thousand years, for the church has Saxon masonry in its low tower. In 1840 Palling had two yawls working from the beach belonging to two separate companies, called the 'Blues' and the 'Whites', but in 1858 the Royal National Lifeboat Institution took over and in 1864 placed the lifeboat *Parsee* there, kept in a boathouse in the sandhills. In 1870 the Number Two lifeboat station was opened, the Number One boat being named the *British Workman*, which gained fame on 7 February 1875 when she went to the aid of a schooner, *Zouvre*, of Portsmouth, which was aground on Happisburgh Sands. In heavy seas she reached the wreck and took off the six-man crew, but no sooner had she landed them safely than she was called out again to go to the assistance of the brigantine *Lisbon* – a double service in which the *British Workman* was at sea for fourteen hours. After motor boats began to make their appearance, the two stations were closed down in 1930. Sea Palling, as it is now called, is very popular with weekend motorists enjoying the fine sandy beach and sea bathing.

Morston is more or less a stepping stone to Blakeney, being in a stretch of fields and marsh land going to the sea. A fourteenth-century squat-looking church greets one on entrance to the village, and rickety walkways lead to Blakeney Point. This well-known bird sanctuary is where visitors are amazed at finding, and seeing, birds laying eggs in the sand without a nest! Blakeney itself has a charm of its own, with winding narrow streets and a pleasing quayside, where pleasure boats cluster waiting for suitable tides – the quay is a favourite haunt of the younger generation, who spend hours and hours catching crabs, most having a bucket full at the end of their efforts, only to empty them into the river again. It is now a motorists' Mecca. Blakeney's nearby neighbours, Cley and Salthouse, are little gems for the artist and the photographer and the bird lover as well. Cley is favoured with a picturesque windmill, which has been featured in many films and on television, the best being *A Conflict of Wings*. Six hundred years ago found it a very prosperous place when Flemish wool buyers were as frequent visitors as the local English merchants and shippers. It has a historic atmosphere, probably owing to its fourteenth-century church, where a fifteenth-century font stands on two high steps. There is also an Elizabethan chest with iron bands, and there are pictures of ships scratched on seats by Elizabethan boys, who, not content with spoiling the seats, had to make more scratchings on the back of the old chancel screen – fans of Francis Drake?

Salthouse suffered greatly in the 1953 coastal sea surge, which inundated most of the east coast from Lincolnshire to Canvey Island. Many lives were lost, farmland flooded, and thousands of shops and houses were under water. Seaside piers and promenades were smashed to pieces, rivers polluted, drains and sewers put out of action and ships actually lifted from rivers and crushed on to hard quay headings. Nelson's jetty at Yarmouth, for example, was almost completely broken up. One of many marine casualties was the *Olcades*, a large oil tanker which came ashore at Walcott after being stranded at Bacton. She was the largest vessel ever to come ashore on the Norfolk coast – 430 feet long, 57 beam, and 26.5 freight. Her immense bulk dwarfed the hundreds of sightseers who came to see her stranded. All around her was the filth and mud, black in places, thrown up by the sea; as if a great plough had run amok.

One

The Broads

The peace and quiet of a morning seventy years ago. This picture was taken on 30 July 1910. This wherry-cum-houseboat has the appearance of being a former lifeboat. What a vast

difference the years have made – then no bungalows and no chalets. No sheds, no factories, no motor cruisers, nor thousands of holiday trippers, as there are today.

Echo of a famous comedian's death. George Formby, the famous Lancashire comedian, whose sudden death left a vacant spot in the theatre world, spent much of his time on the Norfolk Broads. Here is his well-known cruiser, *Lady Beryl*, at Wroxham, with his wife, Beryl, on the bank. The successor to this cruiser (*Lady Beryl II*), was put up for sale by tender by the executors of George's estate.

Becalmed on Wroxham Broads. Just the lap-lap of water on the ship's sides and the swan waiting for titbits. This photograph was taken in 1958 from another yacht.

A quiet backwater at Wroxham, the yachtsman's mecca.

A peaceful scene taken at Wroxham, with one of the modern motor cruisers making for the open Broads.

Sailing time at Horning, famous for its regatta day.

Yachting at Horning, 1950. A typical sailing cruiser as used on the Norfolk Broads. The five miles of river between Wroxham Bridge and Horning Ferry are the busiest in all Broadland.

Yachts, cruisers, geese and ducks at Horning Ferry.

A peaceful scene on the Staithe, Thurne.

Peace and serenity at Thurne – but it could be a death trap if one stepped overboard.

Holidaymaking at Thurne. But none of the crew are wearing life-jackets – one slip, and "finished"!

Yachting at Potter-Heigham.

Old-style dress for cruising up the river, bowler hat and all! The Broads, photographed in 1909. It has been stated that in another hundred years the Broads will cease to exist, through silt and overgrowth with weeds.

The ancient bridge at Potter Heigham, now preserved, carries the Yarmouth road over the river Thurne.

Looking towards Marsh Road, Potter Heigham, in 1950.

Milking time near Potter Heigham. Cows blocking the road, a common sight in Norfolk.

Dove Barn, Potter Heigham, the scene of Methodist anniversaries.

The aptly-named Horsey (Horse-y) drainage windmill of the 'tower' variety, taken in 1949. Horsey has an ancient history dating from Boadicea's time, which knew it as an island, and the Romans, who made it a settlement.

An early spring arrival, Wroxham.

A feed for Dobbin. An appealing photograph of children feeding the horses after the day's work. It is of Doreen Hutson of Main Road, Filby, where the picture was taken.

Harvest aftermath! After the reaping and gathering in, the necessary muck spreading to fertilise the good earth. Here is Mr J. Bean of Main Road, Clippesby, busy at the job.

Picturesque village street, Ludham. The nearby hall was once the home of the poet William Cowper's mother.

Tulip time. A wayside stall at Wayford Nurseries near Stalham. These flower sellers were dotted at intervals along Norfolk's many winding roads.

Music near the river on a Sunday afternoon in 1950. The Stalham Band are playing selections on the green at Potter Heigham – how nice for the yachtsmen and holidaymakers!

Two

Scratby to Cromer

The Coastguard! An interesting relic of the last war – part of an old anti-aircraft gun and the barge *Glenway* which ran ashore at Scratby.

Deserted beaches. A study of the autumn sun reflecting from the sands and marram grass at Winterton, with just a few late holidaymakers having a last look round.

Away from it all! The quiet charm and natural sand dunes of Winterton are in complete contrast to its neighbour Yarmouth. Here two holidaymakers are seen examining the nets used for 'long shoreing'. Apart from the dresses, the photograph could have been taken in Dickens' time.

The straggling sand dunes at Winterton with the now dismantled lighthouse on the left of the picture, and the village on the right. 1945.

The stranded Lowestoft trawler, *IRA*, at Waxham, eventually towed off by the tug *Hector Read*.

The stranding of the French trawler *St Pierre Eglise* at Waxham during a snow storm, 13 February 1955. The *St Pierre Eglise* created a record by being stranded for 55 days before being pulled off by two Dutch tugs on 13 February 1955.

A whale washed ashore at Waxham, 1971. A bulldozer was used to dig a hole to bury the carcass.

The Dutch coaster *Sirius* aground near Sea Palling, September 1949. Late holidaymakers are enjoying the rare sight of a vessel stranded close by on the shore.

A Sea Palling pub with the nautical name of 'The Lifeboat'.

Sea Palling. Wrecked houses are reflected in the pools caused by the sea's flooding in 1953. Many lost their lives here.

'Poppyland'. A round tower of Norfolk, Eccles Tower, which collapsed in a gale on 23 January 1895. The whole town was destroyed in the early 1600s and for hundreds of years the solitary church tower remained, until blown down in a gale on 23 January 1895.

Happisburgh lighthouse, pronounced 'Haisbro'. This lighthouse was featured in one of Anneka Rice's challenges on BBC television. The light is now run by the villagers and not by Trinity House, as of old.

The road to the sea, 1946, before the arrival of the North Sea Gas industry. A pleasing study of the Norfolk countryside, showing the harvest fields and the bungalows and sea approaching Bacton, and the then new Anglia road car.

The years in between! The Gap, Bacton, some forty-five years ago. Then a desolate place with concrete pillboxes and anti-invasion blocks still in evidence, it is now a hive of industry with North Sea Gas.

Bacton, with its new sea wall for coast defence.

A typical Norfolk landscape: a windmill and harvest fields at Paston, near Sheringham.

Paston Windmill when an 'Up for Sale' notice appeared on its fencing. The mill belonged to the McDougal flour family. Also note the new 1948 Ford Anglia on one of its first runs.

On the road to Mundesley, 1949. The picturesque lanes, the sheaves of corn, and the hedges, are now just a memory. The Ford Anglia car was the first in Norfolk to be fixed with 'trafficators'. Formerly, drivers had to put their arms out of the window to indicate turning left or right!

Countryside near Mundesley.

The 'Green' and car park, Mundesley, well patronised by Sunday motorists.

Mundesley Church, after many restorations, is a church without a tower, but it retains a 600-year-old window by the porch.

Picking buttercups and daisies at Denver Mill, Downham Market, a Norfolk mill with a Lincolnshire 'cap'.

Giving a hand stacking the sheaves at harvest time, Mundesley.

The sea shore, Mundesley.

Leading in the winner at Mundesley, 45 years ago.

Part and parcel of a seaside holiday at Mundesley, 1948 – a ride on the donkeys! Here, a young rider seems safe and secure in a basket-like saddle. All ready for that gallop along the sands?

A children's paradise, hunting for crabs and shrimps. Cromer, 1949.

Low tide at Cromer usually means a happy hunting ground for youngsters catching small crabs, starfish, and shrimps.

Deserted beach, Cromer.

The lone yachtsman! The famous yachtsman Sir Alec Rose with Andy and Julie, the author's grandchildren, at Cromer.

Cromer Beach, 1980, with crab boats and crab and lobster pots in the foreground. This type of vessel is unique to Norfolk.

River and sea – an unusual photograph of Cromer. Almost the width of a river or a miniature boating lake, this cavity has been filled in by the sea after excavations for repairing the sea wall.

Cox Henry Blogg of Cromer with the rescued Pyrennean mountain dog, Monte, rescued from the wrecked *Monte Nevoso* on 14 October 1932.

An unusual-looking lighthouse at Cromer.

A typical seaside 'old salt', Henry 'Shrimp' Davies, a former coxwain of the Cromer lifeboat, posing with his crab boat on Cromer beach. He received the nickname 'Shrimp' because when he was born his uncle, the famous lifeboatman Henry Blogg V.C., came to see him; seeing the small bundle in the mother's arms he said, 'what a little shrimp!' and Davies has been known as such right to the present day and was even so named in a BBC interview.

The old sailing and pulling Cromer lifeboat.

Three

Around Sheringham

Autumn shadows at East Runton – the beauty and charm of a north Norfolk resort. A little gem, East Runton is not unlike many Devon and Cornwall holiday haunts with cliffs, sandy beaches, bathing tents and huts, and fishing boats – yet near to the big towns.

An unposed photograph of the jovial fisherman cum chairman cum tent hirer, Mr W. Green of East Runton, looking out for 'sitters' in the fast shortening summer season.

East Runton, July 1954. A popular holiday retreat without the razzmatazz of the larger resorts.

'Any fish, mister?' This photograph was taken at East Runton.

Ye Village Inn, garden and lawn, West Runton.

Felbrigg Hall, near Cromer, with Mr Ketton-Cremer on the left (arms folded) and some of the members of the Norwich Writers' Circle. Felbrigg, bequeathed to the nation by Mr Ketton-Cremer, is now owned by the National Trust and houses the famous library of seventeenth- and eighteenth-century books which belonged to Dr Samuel Johnson.

A rare photograph of Mr Ketton-Cremer at Felbrigg Hall, with the author Mr Mansfield on the right.

A bird's eye view of the Sheringham line. Here a steam train puffs along the open and wooded landscape of north Norfolk, taking holidaymakers and commuters to the resorts of Sheringham and Cromer.

A pretty corner of north Norfolk, near Sheringham, and named as such – Pretty Corner! An ideal spot for a picnic, and popular with weekend motorists.

Sunshine and shadow. An unusual picture of Sheringham, leading up to Beeston Hill with a stormy sun giving strong lighting effects to the buildings.

Jackdaw's holiday! An amusing interlude to the normal holiday fare was the antics of this jackdaw, which made itself at home by flying around in circles and alighting on the back of beach chairs, or onto the beautifully permed heads of the ladies much to their consternation and the delight of bystanders, who appreciated the temporary scare and look of embarrassment

on their faces. Of course, the kiddies were delighted at this diversion from their sand-building and paddling. There was no semi-nudity on the sands in those days – men wore trousers and braces.

'The fishermen of England'! Fishermen mending their nets and crab pots on the Promenade, an interesting sight for summer visitors.

Old salts – Sheringham fishermen sampling the air, *c*. 1950. A good advertisement for the bracing air of the East Coast are these two old fishermen, seen basking in the sunshine on the Promenade at Sheringham. They are Mr Abraham Cooper, aged 93, and Mr J. West, aged 85, both of Sheringham.

A dangerous pastime, climbing the high cliff wall at Sheringham.

Heave ho! How the *J.C. Madge* looked and was launched in 1934. Strong arms and muscles were needed for this job, and these men not only pulled it onto the sand from its shed; they had to push it as well, to get it into the sea! The *J.C. Madge* is now a private yacht – and a tractor would be used to launch it. The *J.C. Madge* (1904–36) cost £1,436 and saved 58 lives. It was decommissioned in 1936; in 1989 the Sheringham Museum Trust bought it, and had it converted to its original state (as seen in the photo) at a cost of £25,000. It is now on show at Weybourne.

Sheringham fishermen hauling up their crab boat. Note that most are wearing Guernsey sweaters.

Sunbathing, sea trips, paddling, and sand modelling, all in one picture, taken in 1949. Note also the large stone pebbles, used for building purposes.

Sheringham.

The beach and gangway, Sheringham.

A hive of industry at Sheringham, a kiddies' paradise for paddling, bathing, and the making of sand castles.

The end of the day, 1953. An unusual against-the-light study of the tents and promenade at Sheringham, taken just after a shower of rain.

The golf links, Sheringham.

Love's young dream on the cliff top at Sheringham.

Four

Weybourne to Wells

The windmill at Weybourne, 1944, now derelict.

A typical post office and stores: Kelling post office.

An African setting in Norfolk. Flamingoes and their island round-house, taken at the aviaries at Kelling Holt.

Kelling Sanatorium.

In the grounds of Kelling Sanatorium, near Holt.

The D'Oyle Carte wing at Kelling Sanatorium, named after the famous opera company.

Salthouse, a nature reserve on the north Norfolk coast, now a preserve for wildfowl. Salthouse was a casualty in the great 1953 sea surge which destroyed houses and land.

Salthouse. No, not bombs – just the fury of the seas! Houses at Salthouse after the 1953 flooding.

Salthouse, showing some of the houses damaged by the floods – note the one cut in half. Thirty-four houses were swept away and every house in the village suffered damage.

Coast sentinel – the tower mill at Cley, 1948. Note the unusual addition of chimneys. Cley windmill has often been used as a 'backcloth' for film companies, the most notable production being *The Conflict of Wings*.

Almost a Dutch landscape. Cley mill from an unusual angle.

Blakeney windmill, 1909. According to Mr Rex Wales, this is the only photograph showing Blakeney mill as it was in its heydey.

Derelict windmill. Blakeney as it is today.

Blakeney is a popular Norfolk yachting centre.

A fascinating pastime at Blakeney Quay – catching crabs with a piece of string baited with a whelk. This youngster caught 102 crabs, only to return them afterwards to the muddy stream.

Blakeney: where the sea meets the town. A popular yachting hide-out, and where the tide once flooded the town and wrecked the small fishing craft.

The fair at Blakeney, 1935.

An old draw well at Blakeney. The water from the well had to serve all purposes.

A September casualty at Blakeney. Another Dutch coaster, the *Karanan* of Rotterdam, comes to grief on this 'dumping ground of Neptune' – the north Norfolk beaches – on 20 September 1936.

Blakeney Church, formerly used as a lighthouse. A brazier burned in the tower to warn shipping.

The font and interior of Blakeney church.

The church on the hill. The bold aspect of the Morston church as seen by motorists passing on their way to Blakeney and Wells.

The bridge of sighs? Some of the members of the Norwich and District Photographic Society, negotiating a rather rickety bridge over the swampy ground at Morston on their annual outing to Blickling Hall and Blakeney Point. Here, they are wondering if the bridge will collapse or who will lose their balance …

Leaving Morston, bound for Blakeney Point.

Whatever are they doing? A baby tern causes these photographers to 'get down to it'. They were among a large number of members of the Norwich and District Photographic Society, who visited Blakeney for their outing. Cameras are not allowed in the National Trust's main ternery so the photographers concentrated on nests and young birds outside its boundaries.

A tern's eggs laid in the sand, Blakeney. Note that there is no nest; the birds just lay their eggs in the sand!

Norwich Photo Society at Blakeney Point looking at terns' eggs just laid on the sand. Again, no nests.

Bird sanctuary, Blakeney Point. The bleak and desolate coast of Blakeney Point is well illustrated in this view of the sand dunes, with footprints of its many visitors. 'Nests' of terns' eggs are frequently seen in batches of two or three and sometimes four. The eggs are laid amid the marram grass, or fully exposed on the sand!

The warden at Blakeney Point – Ted Eales and Sue!

The quiet beauty of a north Norfolk paradise. Paradise Island, Wells – almost a South Sea island picture. This photograph was taken just prior to the 1953 flooding, when the sea inundated the land, washing away the stalls and the cliffs. Many day trippers just come to gather bags and bags of cockles, others to pick samphire, that tasty morsel for the table.

Motorbike trials near Wells.

'High and Dry'. A former 'M.T.B.' used by the Sea Scouts at Wells – lifted up by the abnormal tide in 1953, and deposited on the railway line of Wells' quayside.

The new Wells lifeboat, *The Doris M. Mann of Amphil*, with her crew after a demonstration run. The new lifeboat was named in a ceremony performed by HRH the Duchess of Kent in July 1990. The lifeboat at Wells was the very last to be towed from its shed and launched by horses.

Before the 1953 floods, once a picturesque picnic spot, this is now a car park. This picturesque scene at Wells, familiar to many motorists parking their cars in the woods, is now but a memory. The salt water from the 1953 great sea surge on the East Coast from the Humber to Canvey Island killed these lovely trees. Now not one of them is left.

Just five years between ... ! Look well at these two pictures. yes, they are of the same place, taken from almost the same angle, and have the same 'model' (plus a few years!) and yet, what a difference! The photographs are of that popular retreat, Abraham's Bosum, at Wells. One was taken in 1952, the other a few years later, all the fine trees that once made this site so picturesque having been killed by salt water.

This photograph taken in 1908 shows girls' dress typical of the period.

A general view of Wells.

'Cor! It's thirsty weather on Wells beach'!

Cockles and cockles all alive O. Seafood for the asking – free. No visit to that picturesque little seaside village of Wells would be complete without first trying to gather a bag, or basketful, of delicious cockles when the tide is out. It is a dirty job, as the creatures are buried deep, in thick black mud – and arms and legs are soon covered in the stuff. This photograph was taken in the 1960s.

Five

Burnham to Castle Rising

Old cottages and malt houses at Burnham Overy, now taken over by the National Trust.

Horatio Nelson, born in Burnham Thorpe, as a young man.

Stacking at Burnham Overy, 1950.

Harvest time at Burnham Windmill.

Always popular at the seaside and a 'must' on holiday, for the kiddies – a donkey ride. Here is a typical scene taken on the sands at Hunstanton.

Donkeys at Hunstanton. Note also the long pier, since totally destroyed by rough seas.

In honour of the flood victims. This effective memorial was erected in the gardens on the front at Hunstanton in memory of those who lost their lives in the January 1953 flooding of the East Coast. It also includes the names of sixteen Americans. Of note is the pier in the left hand background which no longer exists after gale damage.

A novel idea for a children's playground, Hunstanton, May 1978. Climbing frames and cowboys and Indians – all very realistic.

Castle Rising, in the past the scene of invasion. Here it is invaded by some of the members of the Norwich and District Photographic Society on their annual holiday – with a battery of cameras.

The ruins of Castle Acre. The castle was built by William de Warenne (who married William the Conquerer's daughter) on the site of an old Roman camp. Norfolk has many interesting ancient ruins.

The ruins of Castle Acre.

The royal estate of Sandringham. Here are the ornamental gardens, with goldfish and lily pond. This stately mansion was opened for the first time in May 1977 to allow visitors to see the contents of the stately rooms.

The famous Norwich gates on the royal estate, Sandringham. Souvenir hunters break off the 'leaves' and take them home as a memento of their visit!

The extensive grounds of Sandringham showing the lake and the host of trees and shrubs.

The grounds of Sandringham Gardens at their best.

What a queue! Part of the large crowd queuing up to get into Sandringham, mainly from motor coaches.

Six

Rural North Norfolk

Sunday at North Walsham. The quaint market cross.

Rustic beauty in a country town. A great attraction of the country towns of Norfolk is the rural beauty, which is so often to be found in their very heart. Here is a glimpse of Aylsham – taken from its churchyard.

The Street, North Elmham. This was the ancient roadway that many a great ecclesiastic and layman took to reach the old Saxon cathedral from AD 673 to 1075.

Wayside refreshment! A handy place of call, the combined pub and cafe at Thornham, just twenty miles from Norwich.

Blickling Hall, one of the finest Jacobean mansions in England. Before the Hall was built in the seventeenth century, the Manor of Blickling stood on the site. The Manor once belonged to the Saxon King Harold, but after Harold's defeat in battle in 1066, William the Conqueror took possession and granted it to his chaplain. Successively it passed through many families. The Erpingham family (see page 112) held it, at another time the Fastolphs; it was owned by Anne Boleyn's grandfather and then, finally, it was granted to Sir Henry Hobart, who built Blickling Hall as we see it today. The Hall has featured many times in films and television.

The library of Blickling Hall.

The front and entrance of Blickling Hall.

Erpingham Church, which takes its name from an ancient family. Thomas Erpingham led the English archers at Agincourt, and erected an imposing 'gate' at the entrance to Norwich Cathedral as a thank-you offering for his deliverance in 1420.

The interior of Erpingham Church.

Easter is usually the first opportunity enabling the public to leave the grime and smut of cities and towns and make for the coast or countryside. Here is a picturesque view of a fine specimen of an unspoilt English church – St Lawrence, Ingworth, built 1390–1400. Many come from miles abroad just to view and inspect this church, which is considered to be a 'true representation of an unspoilt English church'. Note the thatched roof.

The ruins of Binham Priory, near Sheringham, founded over 800 years ago but left ruinous after the Dissolution of the Monasteries.

The ruins of Binham Priory.

The ornate font at Binham Priory.

The Easter pilgrimage to Walsingham. Pilgrims marching with a large, heavy wooden cross to the pilgrimage of the Holy Shrine at Walsingham in 1945. The railway crossing gates are now gone.

'Oliver Twist?' (all of a twist!) Do you remember this church with a crooked spire? It is a well-known church in Norfolk – you cannot think where it is? It is Walsingham Church, photographed in 1908. This fourteenth-century building was entirely gutted by fire in 1961.

Reredos in the Anglican pilgrimage church at Walsingham, showing the Annunciation scene in beautiful colours. The Archangel Gabriel is bringing news to the Blessed Virgin that she is to be the mother of Christ.

A Christmas card scene of Saxthorpe.

A Dickensian village. This photographs shows the war memorial and quaint houses and cottages at Edgefield.

Black-faced lambs making a fine pastoral study. This photograph was taken near Edgefield Holt.

Gathering lavender in the lavender fields, Hunstanton.

Reflections of Stody Lodge in the adjacent pool.

Admiring a picturesque corner of Stody Gardens, now open to the public.

Twyford Hall.

The waterfalls, Swanton Morley.

Countryside in winter – approaching Holt, 1951.

The market place of Holt, an ancient north Norfolk town.

Icy roads at Holt.

The water tower and shopping place, Holt. The water tower has since been removed.

Gresham School, Holt.

The new pedestrian bridge, Holt.

Harvest country! Guist village clock was erected in 1935 by Sir Thomas Cook, commemorating the twenty-fifth anniversary of the ascension of King George V and Queen Mary. Guist is a model village laid out by the family of Thomas Cook & Son.

Country lanes as they used to be, near Guist. Note the new Anglia, fresh from the manufacturer.

The quiet charm of Beeston, which for its size has a surprisingly big church. It was built in the fourteenth century, but a new tower and spire were added in 1873 after it had been struck by lightning.

Cody's touring circus on Beeston Common.

'Goodbye sea – until another year'. Back home tomorrow!